BOG
BOOK

*"I've never written
so much about crap
in my entire life."*

Lou Rolls, 1993.

"What a load of ballcocks."

The Publisher, 1993.

The Bog Book

Take That Books is an imprint of
Take That Ltd.
P.O.Box 200
Harrogate
HG1 4XB

ISBN 1-873668-25-2

Layout, cartoons and typesetting by
Impact Design, P.O.Box 200, Harrogate, HG1 4XB.

Printed and bound in Great Britain.

The Bog Book

FAMOUS BUMS
Neil Bowelstrong

It's one small dump for man.

Find the location of this convenience.

Start at the top left corner and move one square at a time
until you have found the position of this pan.
You may move horizontally, vertically or diagonally.

B	T	Y	I
S	A	N	L
C	O	G	Q
K	D	K	P

Answer: Bangkok

THOMAS CRAPPER

was the inventor of the modern flush toilet.

WARNING
BAD TASTE JOKE

What type of pizzas can you find in your toilet?
Deep pan.

What type of pizzas can you find in your toilet after a couple of days?
Thin and crispy.

Doctor. Doctor. I'm feeling rather flushed.

CRAPPIE

...or *Pounoxis Annularis* is a North American fresh water fish from the central regions and it belongs to the Sunfish family.

The Bog Book

Most people know that claustrophobia means the fear of enclosed spaces - like being shut in the bog all day long. But what about the following fears?

1. Phobophobia
2. Noctophobia
3. Categelophobia
4. Opthalmophobia
5. Triskaidekaphobia
6. Ergophobia
7. Ailurophobia

Fear of... 1.Fear itself, 2.The night, 3.Ridicule, 4.Being stared at, 5.Thirteen, 6.Work, 7.Cats.

A woman goes to the doctor complaining about a pain in the bum. The doctor tells her to take her trousers off, which she promptly does. The doctor has a prod around and pulls out a rose. He looks a bit closer and then pulls out another rose, and another, and another, and another... "Look," said the doctor "I've found a dozen red roses. Do you know how they got there". "No," said the woman "is there a card with them?"

Did you know...

The tomato is not a vegetable? It's a fruit - a love apple.

The largest lake in Africa is Lake Victoria.

The USA is the world's biggest exporter of grain.

Duralumin is an alloy of aluminium and copper used to make aircraft bodies.

The Montgolfier brothers built the first hot air balloon to carry a person.

The Bog Book

Unscramble these seven bathroom items to complete the flush.

1. tepcra
2. knis
3. nisba
4. urshbhttoo
5. hresow
6. romrir

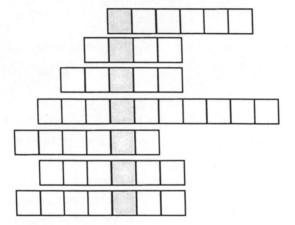

ROLL AROUND IN LAUGHTER AT THIS ONE!

A man comes home late from the office to another burnt meal. "How many times have I told you not to be late for a meal?" said his wife. "To which he replied, "I don't know, I thought you were keeping the score."

The Bog Book

Reach For The Chain.

A little old man walked into a pub, but before he could get to the bar he slipped on some excrement.

Unhurt, he picked himself up, cleaned his shoes, bought a pint and sat at a table by the window.

A couple of minutes later a huge rugby player walked into the bar and slipped on the excrement.

"I just did that!" sniggered the old man.

The rugby player punched him on the nose.

Did you know...

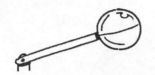

The mouse-eared bat is the only mammal capable of true flight.

Polar bears can run up to 35 miles (56Km) an hour.

Lobsters' blood is pale blue.

The thigh bone is the longest bone in the body.

The first European printed book was the bible printed in Germany.

It takes three years to paint the Forth bridge in Scotland.

Did you hear about the man who kept his wife under the bed at night?

He thought she was a little potty.

The Bog Book

THAT'S A CISTERN FACT

Save Your Bog Roll

For every tonne of waste paper that is collected and re-used, two trees are saved.

BOGWORD 1

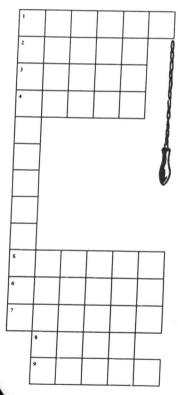

Down
1. Where would you find the bowl?

Across
1. Together.
2. Opposite of always.
3. Francis _____ born in 1543.
4. Come in.
5. Measured in Joules.
6. Worn by train spotters.
7. Homeless people.
8. Explosive eruption from the rear end.
9. Pull it to finish.

WARNING
BAD TASTE JOKE

A man went to meet his girlfriend's parents.
Just as they were sitting down to a meal, he felt a small
fart creep out of his trousers. The smell gradually wafted
around the room and the girlfriend's father looked dismayed.
The man feared the worst, but to his relief the father kicked the
dog which was sitting underneath the man's chair. "Fido, leave
the room now" said the father. Fido didn't move.

Later in the meal the man couldn't help himself and another
silent-but-smelly left his trousers. Again, the father looked
disgusted and kicked the dog. "Fido," he said, "leave the room."
Fido didn't move.

The meal finished without any more disturbances. But just as the
man stood up, another odour emanated from his pants. This time
the man looked straight at the dog and waited for the father to
admonish it once again. "Fido, I've told you before" said the father
"get out of the room before this dirty bugger craps on your head!"

BOG BURIALS

Many ancient human remains have been found in
European bogs. The soft tissues had been preserved
by the waterlogged, anaerobic conditions.
Known finds have been from
Denmark (166), Germany (215),
and Britain (120).

The Bog Book

FAMOUS BUMS
Horatio Nelbum

England expects
everone do do
their business.

FLUSHING

...is a seaport in Zeeland province of West Netherlands
at the mouth of the Schelde river. The Dutch
call it Vlissingen and in 1984 the population
was 46,150.

ROLL AROUND
IN LAUGHTER
AT THIS ONE!

*What was the last thing to
go through the fly's mind
when it hit the car
windscreen?*

Its bum.

THINKS...
*You are not ignorant,
unless somebody
finds out*

The Bog Book

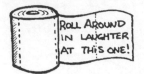

How many Californians go to the toilet at the same time?
25 - one to do the business and 24 to share the experience.

BOGS FOR SALE

Toilets are cheap today,
Cheaper than yesterday.
Small ones are half a crown,
For standing up or lying down.
Big ones are four and six,
For those of you with bigger dicks,
Toilets are cheap today.

Did you know...

A flash of lightening has a voltage of around 100 million Volts.

A household battery has a voltage of around 1.5 Volts.

Resistance to electrical current is measured in Ohms.

Electrical current is measured in Amps.

One Amp passing through a resistance of
one Ohm will create a potential
drop of one Volt.

The Bog Book

THE APPLIANCE
OF SCIENCE

Archimedes discovered that a jobby, when immersed in
water will displace its own volume of water.
If you would like to work out the volume of your latest job,
mark the inside of your bog with a depth indicator. Don't
forget that an equal volume will be displaced on the other
side of the U-bend when making your calculation.
You can also weigh the volume of water displaced. This will
be equal to the difference between the weight of your excreta
in air and the weight in water.

Find the location of this convenience.

Start at the top left corner and move one square at a time
until you have found the position of this pan.
You may move horizontally, vertically or diagonally.

C	A	L	B
A	M	C	X
R	N	U	T
D	I	A	T

Answer: Calcutta.

The Bog Book

INTERNATIONAL TRANSLATOR

English	German	French	Hungarian
Toilet	Abort	Toilette	Mosdó
Bog roll	Klosettpapier	Rouleau	Vécépapír
Urine	Harn	Urine	Fáradtvíz
Shit	Sheisse	Merde	Széklet
Chain	Kette	Chaîne	Lánc
Seat	Platz	Fauteuil	Ülés

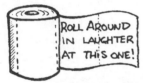
ROLL AROUND IN LAUGHTER AT THIS ONE!

What is brown, steams and comes out of Cowes backwards? *The Isle of Wight ferry.*

What do you call The Bog?

Latrine
Loo
Water Closet
Privy
John
Powder room
Lavatory
Convenience
Urinal
Comfort station
Little boys room

The Bog Book

FAMOUS BUMS
Roll Harris

Have you worked it out yet?

TOP 10 BOG HITS

1. *Waterloo - Abba*
2. *Close the door - Stargazer*
3. *Masterblaster - Stevie Wonder*
4. *Chain Gang - Sam Cooke*
5. *Catch the Wind - Donovan*
6. *Dear John - Status Quo*
7. *Yellow River - Christie*
8. *Writing on the Wall - Tommy Steele*
9. *Oops up side your head - Gap Band*
10. *Pretty Vacant - Sex Pistols*

THINKS...

There is only one clever child in the world - and every mother has it

The Bog Book

CRAPPER CUISINE

Long Brown Log

3 eggs
75 g soft brown sugar
20 ml coffee essence
75 g wholewheat flour
150 ml custard

Put eggs into mixing bowl with sugar. Place bowl in warm water
and whisk until thick and pale. Add coffee essence and whisk.
Fold in flour. Spoon into a tin lined with greaseproof paper.
Bake for 10 minutes on gas mark seven. Sprinkle greaseproof
paper with sugar and turn cake out onto paper.
Roll the cake up loosely from one end.
Mix filling by beating custard with coffee essence.
Unroll cake and spread filling evenly.
Roll back together tightly and serve.

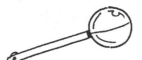

Did you know...

Flushing

is also in the northern part of Queens, New York. Originally a Quaker centre under the control of John Bowne, it became known for its commercial nurseries. These days it is the home of the US Tennis Association's National Tennis Centre. The New York Jets (American Football) and the New York Mets (Baseball) also play in Flushing.

Why does it take a woman with PMT 10 minutes to boil an egg? Because it just bloody-well does O.K.!!

ROLL AROUND IN LAUGHTER AT THIS ONE!

Words that rhyme with:

PONG

strong, dong, bong, gong, long, wrong, prong, throng, song, thong

BEDPAN PRODUCER

Boots the chemist was the biggest producer of bedpans at the turn of the century.

OUR SONIA

This is the tale of Sonia Smell,
To whom an accident befell.
An accident, as will be seen,
Embarrassing in the extreme.

It happened as it does to many,
As Sonia went to spend a penny.
She entered with unconscious grace,
The properly appointed place.

There behind the railway station,
She sat in silent meditation.
Unfortunately not acquainted,
The seat had just been painted.

Too late did Sonia realize,
Her inability to arise.
And though she struggled, pulled, and yelled,
She found she was firmly held.

She raised her voice in desperate shout,
"Please someone come and get me out."
A crowd stood round and slyly sniggered,
And a signalman said, "I'll be jiggered."

"Cor, blimey," said an aging porter,
"We ought to soak her off with water."
The station master and the staff,
Were most polite and did not laugh.

They tugged at Sonia's hands and feet,
But could not remove her from the seat.
A carpenter arrived at last,
And finding Sonia still stuck fast...

Remarked, "I know what I can do,"
And quickly sawed the seat in two.
Sonia stood up, only to find,
She had a wooden halo on her behind.

An ambulance drove down the street,
And took her off complete with seat.
They rushed this pretty gal,
All they way to hospital.

The Bog Book

And holding her hands and head,
Placed her face down on a bed.
The doctors came and cast their eyes,
Upon the seat with some surprise.

A surgeon said, "Now mark my word,
Could anything be more absurd.
Have any of you, I implore
Seen anything like this before?"

"Yes," cried a horny student, unashamed,
"Very often, but never framed."

THAT'S A CISTERN FACT

Domestic bogs are mostly made from porcelain or vitreous china. Public toilets or urinals can be made out of glazed cast iron, steel or stainless steel.

Metric Madness

The metric equivalent of Yards is Metres.
What are the equivalents of the following?:-

1. Pints
2. Miles
3. Ounces
4. Tons
5. Inches

Answers: 1.Litres, 2.Kilometres, 3.Grammes, 4.Tonnes, 5.Centimetres.

*Did you hear about the
elephant with diarrhoea?
No? Well, it's all over
the town.*

The Bog Book

*The bigger the come -
the harder they hit.*

*The bigger they come -
the faster I run.*

*The bigger they come -
the harder you fall.*

MAKING A BOG GARDEN

Water-loving plants such as ferns and primulas can be used to
make a bog garden.

March is the ideal time to construct such a garden. The soil for
the bog garden should be medium or coarse sphagnum peat mixed
with an equal amount of loam. A sprinkling of seaweed fertiliser
will help it get going, but only use around 100g per square metre.
You should place your plants closer together than usual. This
helps the plants keep the ground moist and prevents weeds
from growing.

Plants you could use include: Iris, Astilbe, Hemerocallis,
Plantain Lily, Lysichitum and Primula.

Suitable ferns include: Dryopteris, Blechnum Spicant,
Onoclea Sensibilis, and Scolopendrium.

The Bog Book

FAMOUS BUMS
Queen Victoria

I am not bumused!

*What's worse than coming home from a hard day's work,
to find your spouse sitting in front of a blazing fire?
Coming home to find your spouse sitting in front of a blazing fire
when you don't have a fireplace!*

Did you know...

Most centipedes have less than 100 legs, but some have been known to have over 350.

The first book was printed in China in 868 AD.

There are over 20,000 species of butterfly.

There are still around 20,000 cowboys in America.

Julius Caeser was stabbed in 44 BC.

*Message on the urinal wall;
Did you know you've got wet shoes?*

The Bog Book

BOGWORD 2

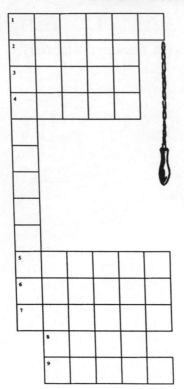

Down

1. Make it go down.

Across

1. Round, lumpy and brown with eyes.
2. Not on top.
3. From nearby.
4. Even, devoid of lumps.
5. Ancient calculator.
6. A fly is an _____.
7. See something.
8. Cow muck.
9. Aroma.

Words that rhyme with:

STINK

ink, kink, chink, jink, link, blink, pink, brink, drink, shrink, sink, think, wink, zinc

THINKS...

We are not all perfect - but some are closer than others

The Bog Book

OLD LADIES

Oh, dear what can the matter be,
Five old ladies got stuck in the lavatory,
They were there from Sunday to Saturday,
Nobody knew they were there.

They said they were going to have tea with the vicar,
They went in together, they thought it would be quicker,
But the lavatory door was a bit of a sticker,
And the Vicar had tea all alone.

The first was the wife of a Deacon in Dover,
And though she was known as a bit of a rover,
She liked it so much she thought she'd stay over,
And nobody knew she was there.

The next lady was old Mrs Tickle,
She found herself in a terrible pickle,
Shut in a pay room, and she didn't have a nickel,
And nobody knew she was there.

The next was the Bishop of Chester's daughter,
Who went to pass some extra water,
She pulled on the chain and the rising water caught her,
And nobody knew she was there.

The next old lady was named Miss Trim,
She'd only sat down on a personal whim,
But somehow got pinched between the pan and the brim,
And nobody knew she was there.

The last old lady was Madam Humphry
Who settled down to make herself comfy,
Then found out she couldn't get her bum free,
And nobody knew she was there.

The Bog Book

Why do turds have tapered ends?

So your bum doesn't snap shut when you release them.

WARNING
BAD TASTE JOKE

Did you know...

The biggest flower is Rafflesia which only flowers once every 10 years.

A giraffe's neck only has seven bones, the same as a human's.

Elizabeth II is the seventh Queen in Britain.

Yorkshire is the largest county in England.

FM on your radio stands for Frequency Modulation.

A pot-holer slipped and fell down a small fissure. His friends rushed out to get help from the nearest village. After several hours a rescue team arrived. They descended to where the pot-holer had fallen and shone a light down. "We're from the Red Cross," shouted a rescuer.

"I gave last week," came the reply.

The Bog Book

FAMOUS BUMS
Humphry Bumgart

Flush it again, Sam.

A Capital Idea

What is the capital of ?:-

1. Mongolia
2. Kenya
3. Saudi Arabia
4. Netherlands
5. Gabon
6. Bolivia

Answers: 1.Ulan Baatar, 2.Nairobi, 3.Riyadh, 4.Amsterdam, 5.Libreville, 6.La Paz.

THINKS...

If Drake wasn't afraid of the Armada, why did he have to play with his bowels?

The Bog Book

This is to certify that

YOUR NAME PRINTED HERE

has been awarded the distinguished honour of

Batchelor of
The Bog Brush
(B.Bog.)

after passing Hard Things in the toilet, such as irrelevant questions. Never again let it be said that this person *probably* has 'shit for brains'. This certificate is absolute proof that they do.

Signed this day _____

Lou Rolls

Lou Rolls,
Author of The Bog Book

BACHELOR OF
THE BOG BRUSH

If you can answer these questions, you qualify for a respected academic qualification - the Bachelor of The Bog Brush. The certificate is unique in not offering you the faintest hope of getting a better jobby - not even in the public loos.
To qualify, simply answer the following questions correctly and send off for your personalised degree certificate (21 cm x 30 cm). Of course, you could ask us to put someone else's name on it! The certificate is printed on quality marbled paper.

1. Who invented the flush toilet?
A) Thomas the Toilet
B) Thomas Crapper
C) Thomas Bog
D) John Thomas

2. Is Flushing...?
A) A seaport in West Netherlands.
B) An area in the Bronx, New York.
C) A game played by American Indians.
D) A medical condition in older women.

3. What is a Crappie?
A) A Toilet
B) A game of dice
C) A really poor game of football
D) A North American fish

4. What is Ergophobia the fear of ?
A) Ergs
B) The product of the frequency of
   oscillation and the Planck constant
C) Work
D) Stupid people

5. How fast can Polar Bears run?
A) Faster than you
B) 56 kilometres and hour
C) 35 miles and hour
D) All of the above

To receive your certificate - in your own or
anybody else's name - write your answers on a
plain piece of paper and send it together with a
cheque for £1.75 (made payable to Take That Ltd.)
to cover printing and postage, to:
Bachelor of the Bog Brush, Take That Ltd.,
PO Box 200, Harrogate HG1 4XB.

- -

YES, I have spent many hours studying The Bog
Book, drunk a lot and generally lazed around (just like
a real student). Therefore I am qualified to receive
𝕿𝖍𝖊 𝕭𝖆𝖈𝖍𝖊𝖑𝖔𝖗 𝖔𝖋 𝖙𝖍𝖊 𝕭𝖔𝖌 𝕭𝖗𝖚𝖘𝖍 certificate.

Please make out a certificate in the name of:

(block capitals) _____

and send it to:

Name: _____

Address: _____

_____

_____

_____ Postcode: _____

The Bog Book

FAMOUS BUMS
Basil Bogbrush

Bum! Bum!

Did you know...

The highest calorie intake per head
of population is in Belgium

The lowest calorie intake per head is in Mozambique.

West Germany had approximately 12 tractors
per square kilometre in 1987.

Switzerland has the highest Gross Domestic Product
per head of population.

Mexico City is the largest city by population.

THINKS...

*Did Winnie the Pooh
wished he'd lost.*

The Bog Book

Gattling Bum

350g yellow split peas
2 onions
50g butter
20 ml lemon juice
50g fennel seeds
3 hard-boiled eggs

Cook peas in water until tender. Fry onions in butter for 10 minutes until browned. Add onions and butter to the peas and mash lightly. Add the lemon juice and season with salt and pepper. Spoon into shallow serving dish and keep warm. Melt remaining butter and fry fennel seeds for 2 minutes until they start to pop. Pour seeds and butter over pea and onion mixture. Quarter the hard-boiled eggs and tuck them round the edge to serve.

What do you do when you go to the bog?

Relieve oneself
Answer the call of nature
Shake hands with the unemployed
See a man about a dog
Make water
Piddle
Pee
Have the runs
Excrete
Go to the lavatory
Move one's bowels
Micturate
Spend a penny

The Bog Book

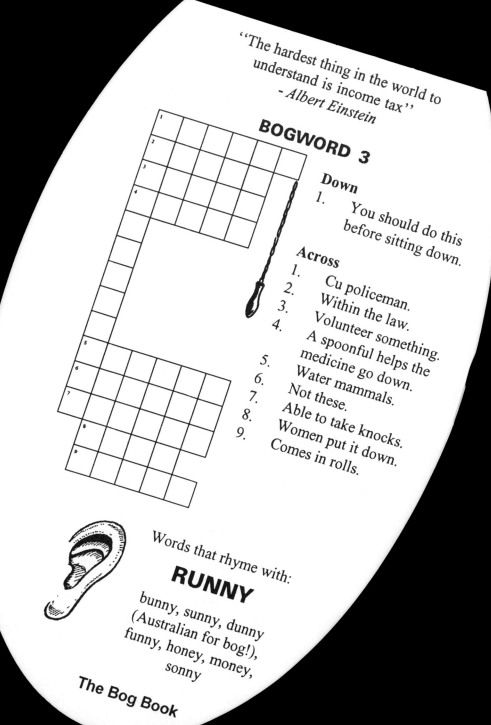

"The hardest thing in the world to understand is income tax"
- *Albert Einstein*

BOGWORD 3

Down

1. You should do this before sitting down.

Across

1. Cu policeman.
2. Within the law.
3. Volunteer something.
4. A spoonful helps the medicine go down.
5. Water mammals.
6. Not these.
7. Able to take knocks.
8. Women put it down.
9. Comes in rolls.

Words that rhyme with:

RUNNY

bunny, sunny, dunny (Australian for bog!), funny, honey, money, sonny

The Bog Book

A Contest of the Wind

Entries are requested for the 69th airing of the **World Farting Championships** to take place at Windy Hole, Nawfuck on Saturday 31st February. Contestants must hold a minimum qualification of 5th dan in *Itchi Bum* in order to be accepted.

THE FOLLOWING RULES WILL APPLY:

1. Make sure the previous contestant has put their weaponry back into their trousers, or run out of ammunition, before mounting the platform.

2. Walk to the middle of the stage and loosen any belts, ties, braces or string used to hold trousers in place.

3. Grasp the Parping Pole with both hands, left above right, and wiggle your backside to reveal your arsehole. Involuntary explosions during this manoeuvre will be penalised. Keep your bum pointing toward the sky until the safety screens have been erected.

4. On the command "Blast" from the panel of judges, lower your bum and commence your farting routine.

5. Silent But Deadlies, Raspers, Blanket Blarps, Earthquakes and Trumpets will be permitted.

6. Cushion Dusters, Thunderclaps and 1812 Overtures are not allowed.

7. Parps, Blips and Squeaks are only allowed in the junior competition.

8. Anyone shitting will be instantly disqualified.

9. Extra points will be awarded for thickness and aroma.

10. Please replace any fixtures and fittings knocked loose before leaving the stage.

The Bog Book

A Contest of the Wind
continued

Entrants should indicate whether they are
entering the Individual, Doubles, Mixed Doubles
or Eleven-a-Side competitions.

A display by the German 'Fart Box' Formation
Farting Team will take place at the end of the
competition while the judges sniff through their notes.

Spectators are warned to bring their own pegs,
safety glasses and helmets.

*A man walked into the doctor's surgery with
a cricket ball firmly stuck up his backside.
"What's wrong with you?" said the doctor.
"I caught a cricket ball up the bum in
Sunday's game" said the man.
"Howzat" said the doctor.*

WORKING DOWN THE SEWER

Working down the sewer,
Shovelling up manure,
That's the way I must do my bit
Shovelling up the shit.
You can hear my shovel sing
With a ting-a-ling-a-ling,
When I'm working down the sewer
With all that man-made manure.

The Bog Book

Size Your Stool

Cut your most recent stool through the point of greatest diameter and compare it to this chart.

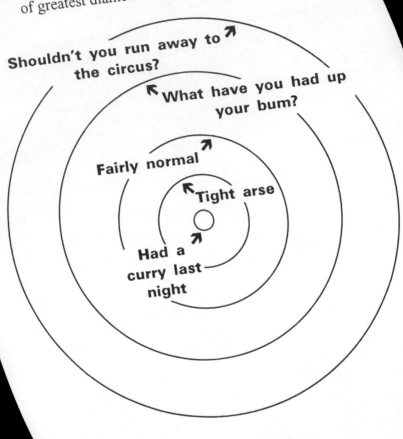

Shouldn't you run away to ↗
the circus?

↖ **What have you had up**
your bum?

Fairly normal ↗

↖ **Tight arse**

↗
Had a
curry last
night

THINKS...

All things come to
he who waits - but
not soon enough!

The Bog Book

FAMOUS BUMS
Nappy Blownapart

What a sight, Josephine.

Find the location of this convenience.

Starting with a letter 'A', move one square at a time
until you have found the position of this pan.
You may move horizontally, vertically or diagonally.

D	A	B	M
A	M	S	A
R	O	T	D
T	M	E	R

Answer: Amsterdam.

*If wit were shit, this book
would be constipated.*

The Bog Book

Did you know...

More than 100,000 ants can live in one colony,
and they will all have the same mother.

Pompeii was destroyed by the eruption
of Vesuvius in 79 AD.

The population of Buenos Aires is approximately 30,500,000.

The population of China is approximately 1,160,000,000.

There are more than 50 alphabets in use around the world.

TOP 10 BOG HITS (II)

1. *This 'ole House - Shakin Stevens*
2. *Born to Run - Bruce Springsteen*
3. *The Shape of Things to Come - Yardbirds*
4. *Shakin All Over - Johnny Kidd and the Pirates*
5. *Wayward Wind - Frank Ifield*
6. *Swing Low - Eric Clapton*
7. *My Little One - Marmalade*
8. *Strange Brew - Cream*
9. *Oldest Swinger in Town - Fred Wedland*
10. *I Missed Again - Phil Collins*

"The wave machine is great, but I think the sewage pipe is going a bit far."

Timely Movements

How many hours ahead of the UK are the following countries?:-

1. Algeria
2. Iceland
3. Chad
4. Peru
5. China
6. New Zealand

Answers: 1. +1, 2. 0, 3. +1, 4. -5, 5. +8, 6. +12.

THAT'S A CISTERN FACT

In 1778, Joseph Bramah (born in England on 13th April 1748) designed and built an improved version of the toilet.

The Bog Book

GAMES TO PLAY
IN THE BOG

Lid Flapper

A game for two people. One person lifts and lowers the lid, whilst his or her opponent must fill the pan. Points are scored for each full second of filling completed. One point is lost for each splash on the lid. The game is immediately forfeited if you splash your opponent.

Sink the Submarine

Leave a solid turd in the pan to settle on the bottom. Return a little later and try to destroy it with a stream of liquid. Sufficient force must be gathered to cause pressure waves to reach down to the 'submarine'.

Fly on the Wall

A test of aim to be played in the summer months. Leave the window open until a couple of unsuspecting flies enter the bog. Close the window and wait for them to hover around the pan. When the do, see if you can shoot them down.

Bombs Away

Quite simple. How high can you stand on the seat and still drop your bombs into the dam?

Rip the Paper

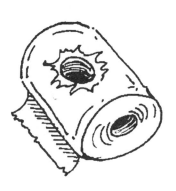

Place a piece of bog-roll on top of the water. Allow it to become sodden, and then try to punch a hole through it with your projectiles. Gradually decrease the time allowed for 'wetting' of the paper the more proficient you become.

Mix and Match

Another game for two participants. The person who is 'it' must intersect their stream with their opponents. If they succeed, 'it' is transferred to the other person and the game continues. The person not being 'it' when both contestants have run out of ammunition is the winner.

Upside Down

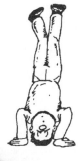

Think it's easy to go to the bog? Then try it while standing on your head. Men will find this easier than women.

The Bog Book

A drunk sat on the pavement in tears and was noticed by a passing vicar. Wanting to help, the vicar wandered over an inquired what the problem was. The drunk explained that he had just swapped his wife for a bottle of whisky. ''Ah,'' said the vicar, ''and now you realise that you really loved your wife and want her back?'' ''No,'' said the drunk, ''now the bottle's empty.''

INCONTINENT WIFE

She is a winsome wee thing,
She is a handsome wee thing,
She is a bonny wee thing,
This sweet wee wife o' mine.
Robert Burns

The oldest known reference to paper for use in the toilet was made in China in 589 AD

Did you know...

The largest cat is the Siberian tiger.

If you mix red and green light you get yellow light.

There are 10 ways of being bowled out in cricket.

An Elephant is pregnant for 22 months.

Everest's peak was first climbed in 1953.

The Bog Book

FAMOUS BUMS
Elvis

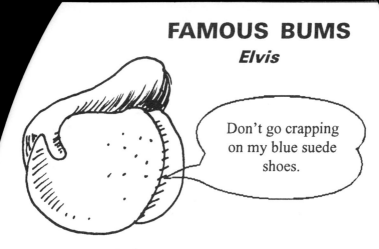

Don't go crapping on my blue suede shoes.

SCHIZOMYCETES
(Bacteria)

Most bacteria are benign and harmless to humans. Those which produce disease are known as pathogens. Unfortunately, human excrement contains a large amount of pathogenic bacteria, so they need to be treated to stop them getting into the domestic water supply.

The breakdown of sewage - containing organic material such as proteins, carbohydrates and fats - requires the use of other, friendly bacteria. Septic tanks, trickle filters and sand filters are all designed to allow this bacteriological battle to take place.

One drop of saliva contains millions of bacteria.

Our company's motto is ''Push'' - it says so on the door.

PUSH

The Bog Book

BOGWORD 4

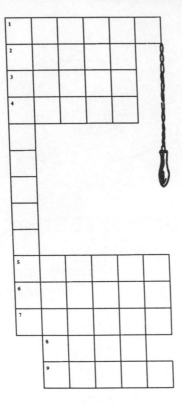

Down

1. Used to kill the germs

Across

1. Times two.
2. Not outer.
3. Begin.
4. Needs a scratch.
5. Sharp.
6. Vital.
7. Favourite drink.
8. Leave behind.
9. Used to flush.

What's caused that pong?

Let rip
Fart
Blow off
Bumblast
Blarp
Chuff
Guff
Pump
Trump
Chadoof

The Bog Book

The batsman's Holding, the bowler's Willy.

Dai O'Rhea	run out	0
N. Continent	caught short	0
Long, Richard	middle stump	0
Nicks A Brown	boweled	0
Jake the Peg	leg before	0
WC Fields	caught flushing	0
Sty Pated	not out yet	0
Sister Itis	retired hurt	0
Total		bog all

To bat: T.Rump, No.10 'Inches', P.All

Did you know...

A proton weighs 2,000 times more than an electron.

A neutron weighs about the same as a proton.

Protons and neutrons are made up of quarks.

Quarks come in many varieties, including 'up', 'down' and 'strange'.

Tachyons travel faster than light.

THINKS...

What you don't know won't hurt you - but it will amuse a lot of people.

The Bog Book

Pre-Bog Wonders

What were the seven wonders of the world?

The Pyramids in Egypt.
The Hanging Gardens of Babylon.
The Temple of Artemis at Ephesus.
The Statue of Zeus at Olympia.
The Mausoleum of Halicarnassus.
The Colossus of Rhodes.
The Pharos of Alexandria.

Words that rhyme with:

BOG

cog, dog, fog, jog, hog,
log, clog, smog, flog,
grog, slog, nog,

*A man came home early one day
from work to find his wife in bed
with another man. "Hey what
are you doing," said the husband.
"See," said the wife to her lover,
"I told you he was stupid."*

Picasso experimented with colours in 1906
to come closer to the sculptured form.
During this period, he painted **La Toilette**.
Born in Spain on 25th October 1881,
Picasso lived most of his life in France
and died there at the age of 91
on 8th April 1973.

The Bog Book

FAMOUS BUMS
Lavvy Grayone

Shit,
that bog door.

Did you know...

Canada has over 65,800 kilometres of railway.

Japanese trains carry each passenger an average of 2,700 kilometres a year.

Turkish trains carry each passenger an average of 120 kilometres a year.

Czechoslovakian trains transport around 68,000 million tonne kilometres of freight.

The old USSR had a total of over 245,000 kilometres of railway.

The Chinese language only has 15,000 words. The problem is, none of them are English.

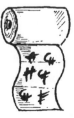

The Bog Book

Yellow River

300 ml fish stock
4 egg yolks
Juice of 2 lemons
50 g of arrowroot
White pepper

Warm the fish stock. Whisk egg yolks and lemon juice
in a basin. Pour some of the warm stock into the mixture.
Whisk and tip back into the stock. Cook gently and
continue to whisk.
Mix arrowroot with two tablespoons of cold water and stir
in three tablespoons of the sauce. Add to the pan of sauce
stirring all the time until it goes smooth and glossy.
Season with pepper and serve.

Find the location of this convenience.

Start at the top right corner and move one square at a time
until you have found the position of this pan.
You may move horizontally, vertically or diagonally.

M	Z	A	H
A	G	R	U
T	O	R	B
E	D	I	N

Answer: Harrogate.

The Bog Book

THAT'S A CISTERN FACT

Sewage was originally transported away from towns in England in buckets and carts. These were then emptied into nearby water-filled ditches which emptied into rivers. During the Industrial Revolution, cities became too large to deal with sewage in this manner. Many households took to emptying their sewage out of a window into the street, causing widespread epidemics of typhoid and dysentery.

WARNING
BAD TASTE JOKE

A native population control programme using oral contraceptives wasn't working at all. So the doctor decided the men would have to be trained to use condoms. The next day a native man came into the surgery who had twelve children and didn't want any more. The doctor promptly produced a condom, and through a translator told him that as long as he always wore it his wife wouldn't become pregnant.

A month later the native came back with his wife who was pregnant. The doctor looked to the heavens for help, and called in the interpreter so he could give the man good telling off.

"Why didn't he wear the sheath," asked the doctor. The translator spoke briefly with the native and then replied "He swears he did wear it."

"Then how on earth did his wife get pregnant?" Again the translator talked with the native. "He says," stuttered the translator, "that after a week he needed a piss so badly that he cut the end off it!"

The Bog Book

PLEASE REFRAIN

Gentlemen should please refrain,
From flushing toilets while the train,
Is standing in the station for a while.
We encourage contemplation,
While the train is in the station,
Cross your legs and grit your teeth and smile.

If you wish to pass some water,
You should sing out for a porter,
Who will place a basin in the bog.
Tramps and wasters underneath,
Get it in the eye and in the teeth,
But that is what comes from being the underdog.

If the Gents' room is taken,
Do not feel the least forsaken,
Never show the sign of sad defeat,
Try the Ladies' across the hall,
And if some lady has felt the call,
She'll courteously relinquish her seat.

Drinking while the train is moving,
Is another way of proving,
That control of eye and hand is sure,
We like our clients to be neat,
So please don't wet upon the seat,
Or worse still, don't splash upon the floor.

If your efforts are in vain,
Then simply break a window pane,
This latest method's used by very few,
So be careful where you aim it,
If you don't get it in the pit,
The wind might blow it back at you.

THINKS...
*Faults are easier to
find in others*

The Bog Book

Panley

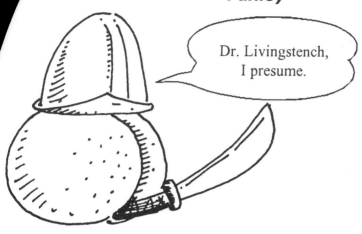

Dr. Livingstench, I presume.

Did you know...

India is the top exporter of tea.

Brazil is the top exporter of coffee.

Ghana is the top exporter of cocoa.

Cuba is the top exporter of sugar.

The US is the top exporter of tobacco.

Sanitary fixture traps, or U-bends, create a water seal between the sewage pipes and the rooms in which bogs are installed.

The Bog Book

THE GORMLESS BOG OF RECORDS

All attempts to gain a place in this bog of records are undertaken at the potential claimants own risk. The publishers of The Bog Book cannot accept responsibility for any pulls, strains, or other disfigurements received while making a record attempt. Claimants should recognise the sheer embarrassment that an entry in this list can cause.

Highest Dump * Climber Ben Down is recognised to hold the record for the dump at highest altitude when he lost his footing while having his photograph taken on top of Everest. Although Ben had to leave his trousers at the laundromat recently opened at base camp, the camera shots clearly show the stains of his achievement.

Biggest * The award for the largest toilet in the world goes to the Asia Republic of Bindia. Apparently the whole country is one big toilet.

Highest Piddle * Jean Claude Repéter filled his lavabo from a height of 4885 metres. Firmly squatting on top of Mont Haute, Jean Claude used carefully selected warm air currents to guide his fluid into the pan of his apartment in the village of Petitpois.

Longest Residence * Management Consultant Mike Tightarse spent 176 hours in the toilet of *The Bull and Duck* in the summer of 1993. A slightly embarrassed Mike came out to receive the award when he discovered it wasn't his round after all.

The Bog Book

A sex therapist started a new class for people who felt they needed 'more'. His first aim was to find out how many times they did it normally. So he asked how many people had sex every night. Four people put their hands up. Then he asked how many did it once a week. Ten people put their hands up. The questioning went on until everybody had put their hands up except one small man in the corner of the room. "How many only have sex once every three months?" said the therapist. The man did not move. "How many only have sex once every six months?" said the therapist. The man did not move. "Ok," sighed the therapist, "How many only have sex once a year?" At this the little man jumped up, put his hand in the air and said "Me, me, me, I do!!" "That's fine," muttered the therapist confused, "but there's no need to get so excited." "Yes there is," said the man, "tonight's the night! tonight's the night!"

APPEAL UPHELD

A court yesterday awarded a toilet cleaner £300,000 compensation for unfair dismissal against his ex-employers. After 25 years working in the toilets Mr Jones, 46, was sacked for spending too long on the bog instead of cleaning them. According to a company representative, Mr Jones spent ''half his life making work for himself.'' Summing up, the judge agreed that Mr Jones had been suffering from Repetitive Bowel Syndrome.

The Bog Book

Did you know...

Benjamin Franklin was the 15th of 17 children.

The mammoth cave system in Kentucky, USA has 345 km (214 miles) of caves and passages.

A red blood cell is only 0.007 mm in diameter.

A drop of blood contains around 100,000,000 red blood cells.

The numbers we use in the English language (1,2,3,4,5,etc.) are called Arabic numbers.

GET UP AND GONE

I'm aware that my youth has been spent
That my get up and go has got up and went.
But I really don't mind, when I think with a grin,
Of all the great places my get up has been.

Pour Elle et Lui

L'eau de Bowl

Blended in our most used toilette by the arses of our most experienced scientists. One small 'dab' behind the ears and on the wrists will attract the classiest of flies. Go on, use your nose, buy a bottle today. (Formulated and controlled by Laboratoire Pongier)

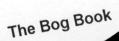

The Bog Book

BOGWORD 5

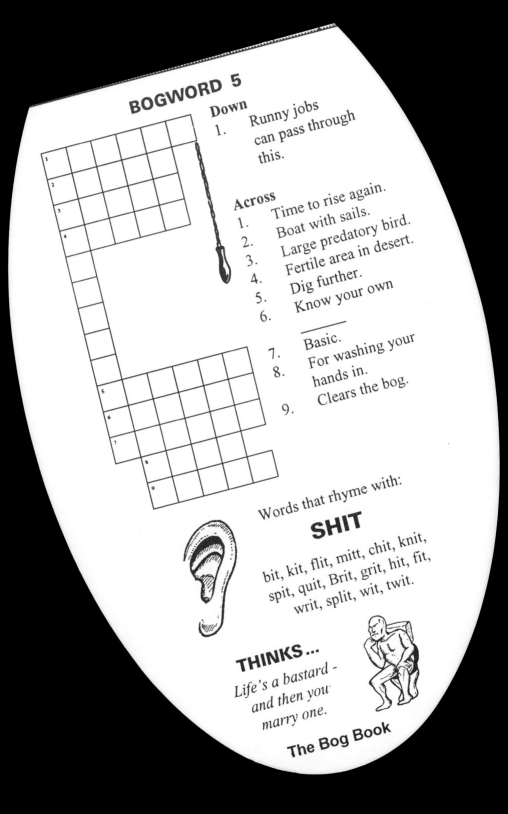

Down

1. Runny jobs can pass through this.

Across

1. Time to rise again.
2. Boat with sails.
3. Large predatory bird.
4. Fertile area in desert.
5. Dig further.
6. Know your own
   ____
7. Basic.
8. For washing your hands in.
9. Clears the bog.

Words that rhyme with:

SHIT

bit, kit, flit, mitt, chit, knit, spit, quit, Brit, grit, hit, fit, writ, split, wit, twit.

THINKS...

Life's a bastard - and then you marry one.

The Bog Book

Did you know...

Over 500 clubs enter the FA cup each year.

A touchdown in American football is worth six points.

There are up to 40 players in an American football team, but only 11 are on the pitch at any one time.

Rugby League broke away from Rugby Union in 1895.

A Rugby Union team contains 15 players and a Rugby League side contains 13 players.

NO USE

Why was he born so beautiful?
Why was he born at all?
He's no bogging use to anyone,
He's no bogging use at all.

What they didn't teach you in French class
(Impress your Au Pair)

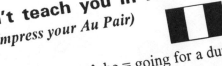

Couler un bronze, or poser sa pêche = going for a dump

Renverser la vapeur = go for a slash

Tirer la chasse = pull the chain

Péter = to fart

Ça pue = it stinks

Le cul = arse

The Bog Book

FAMOUS BUMS
Winstbum Churchill

We shall do it on the beaches.

Find the location of this convenience.

Starting with the letter 'T', move one square at a time
until you have found the position of this pan.
You may move horizontally, vertically or diagonally.

L	O	N	D
A	T	R	I
M	S	T	P
R	I	L	O

Answer: Triploi.

The Bog Book

Balls and Liver

1 onion 1 bayleaf
1 carrot
750 g calves' sweatbreads
Flour & Butter
100 g foie gras
1 truffle 1 shallot
White wine
Chicken stock

Boil onion, bayleaf and carrot in water. Drop in cow's balls and turn down heat for 30 minutes. Cool. Once cool, peel off the thin skin around the balls, lay them in a tin and squash. Cut the flat balls into four portions and flour lightly. Melt butter and fry both sides for 15 minutes. Lay on a thin slice of goose liver. Fry thin slices of truffle with the shallot. Pour in white wine and boil. Add chicken stock and then butter. Strain the sauce over the balls and then scatter the truffle slices. Serve hot enough to dull taste buds.

Warm Blast

What are the usual minimum temperatures (in degrees Celsius) in the following cities during April to June?:-

1. London
2. Los Angeles
3. Cairo
4. Moscow
5. Paris
6. Rio de Janeiro
7. Wellington

Answers: 1.4, 2.10, 3.14, 4.-1, 5.8, 6.18, 7.7.

The Bog Book

ROLL AROUND IN LAUGHTER AT THIS ONE!

Lecturer to student: "Who's your favourite author?"
Student: "My dad."
Lecturer: "What does he write?"
Student: "Cheques!"

THAT'S A CISTERN FACT

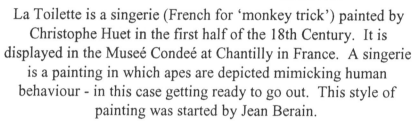

La Toilette is a singerie (French for 'monkey trick') painted by Christophe Huet in the first half of the 18th Century. It is displayed in the Museé Condeé at Chantilly in France. A singerie is a painting in which apes are depicted mimicking human behaviour - in this case getting ready to go out. This style of painting was started by Jean Berain.

THINKS...

Does diarrhoea run in the family?

MY OLD MAN WAS A MINER

My old man was a miner,
He worked all day in the pit,
Sometimes he'd shovel up coal,
Sometimes he'd shovel up shit.

The Bog Book

Little Birdie flying high
Did a whoopsie in the sky
Said the farmer wiping his eye
''Damn good thing cows don't fly''

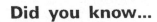

Did you know...

Aborigines now make up less than 1%
of the Australian population.

CFC is short for chloroflourocarbon.

The highest peak in Africa is Mount Kilimanjiro at 5,895 metres.

The largest lake in Africa is Lake Victoria at nearly
69,000 square miles.

Nigeria has the largest population in Africa.

*Dentist to little boy: ''Stop screaming,
I haven't started drilling yet.''
Little boy to dentist: ''I know, but
you're standing on my foot!''*

The Bog Book

Bogs on Film

DID YOU KNOW
1,436 people have been
murdered in the toilet
on the big screen.

Top Five Famous Scenes:

1. **Witness:** A young Amish boy (Lukas Haas) witnesses a murder in the toilet.

2. **The Shining:** A schizophrenic husband (Jack Nicholson) axes down the bog door to get to his wife.

3. **Firefox:** An American pilot (Clint Eastwood), disguised as a businessman, sees off a KGB agent in a Moscow underground toilet.

4. **The Unforgiven:** A hired cowboy killer pumps several shots into his victim who is sitting on the john.

5. **Sleeping with the Enemy:** An oppressed wife (Julia Roberts) feigns death and attempts to flush her wedding ring down the toilet. Her husband finds the ring in the pan, and sets off in pursuit.

"Now it all comes back to me," said the skunk when the wind changed direction.

THINKS...

Why not take a walk into your local tax office - and see the people you are working for.

The Bog Book

Did you know...

Air is 78% nitrogen and only 21% oxygen.

The troposphere contains 90% of the air in the atmosphere.

The first flight by the Wright brothers lasted only 12 seconds and was shorter than the wing-span of a jumbo jet.

Alexander the Great was only 32 when he died in Babylon.

Adult crocodiles can reach 6 metres in length.

"When the loo paper gets thicker and the writing paper thinner it's always a bad sign, at home"
- Nancy Mitford, Love in a Cold Climate.

What do you call that stuff?

Waste matter	Faeces
Stool	Ordure
Shit	Dung
Muck	Droppings
Guano	Cast

Alsop said "Death is, after all, the only universal experience except birth." Did he never go to the bog?

THINKS...

Skiing - by the time you've learnt to stand up, you can't sit down.

The Bog Book

FAMOUS BUMS
George Washingbum

Flush the colon-ists out.

Bogword 1 Answers
Down: Under the seat **Across:** 1.United, 2.Never, 3.Drake, 4.Enter, 5.Energy, 6.Anorak, 7.Tramps, 8.Fart, 9.Chain.

Bogword 2 Answers
Down: Pull the chain **Across:** 1.Potato, 2.Under, 3.Local, 4.Level, 5.Abacus, 6.Insect, 7.Notice, 8.Dung, 9.Smell.

Bogword 3 Answers
Down: Close the door **Across:** 1.Copper, 2.Legal, 3.Offer, 4.Sugar, 5.Otter, 6.Other, 7.Robust, 8.Seat, 9.Paper.

Bogword 4 Answers
Down: Disinfectant **Across:** 1.Double, 2.Inner, 3.Start, 4.Itchy, 5.Abrupt, 6.Needed, 7.Tipple, 8.Dump, 9.Water.

Bogword 5 Answers
Down: Eye of a needle **Across:** 1.Easter, 2.Yacht, 3.Eagle, 4.Oasis, 5.Deepen, 6.Limits, 7.Earthy, 8.Sink, 9.Brush.

I've got a photographic mind - I just can't get it developed.

The Bog Book

THE DOGGIES MEETING

The doggies all held a meeting,
They came from near and far,
Some came by push bike,
Some by motor car.

Each doggy passed the entrance,
Each doggy signed the book,
Then each unzipped their backside,
And hung it on the hook.

One dog was not invited,
It sorely raised his ire,
He ran into the meeting room,
And loudly shouted ''Fire.''

It threw them into confusion,
And without a second look,
Each grabbed another's backside,
From off another hook.

And that's the reason why, sir,
When walking down the street,
And that's the reason why, sir,
When doggies chance to meet,
And that's the reason why, sir,
On land, or sea, or foam,
All doggies sniff another's backside,
To see if it's his own!

THINKS...

*If your foot slips, you can
recover your balance, but if
your bottom slips, you can
not recover the smell.*

The Bog Book

A Wunch of Bankers

Do you HATE BANKS? Then you need this collection of stories aimed directly at the crotch of your bank manager. A Wunch of Bankers mixes cartoons and jokes about banks with real-life horror stories of the bare-faced money-grabbing tactics of banks. If you think you've been treated badly, read these stories!!!! £3.99

The Drinker's IQ Test

Have you ever wondered if drink is affecting your brain? Then this book will confirm your worst fears or give you a clean bill of health. Do you know how much pub crisps work out at per tonne? What would you do if a German gave you two-fingers? How much beer can anybody drink on an empty stomach? And while you are thinking, there's a collection of the world's best drinking jokes to relax your brain. £3.99

How to Get Rid of Your Boss

No matter how much you love your work, there is always one person who makes your professional life a misery - your boss. But all that can change. Find out, with the use of helpful diagrams and cartoons, how to get rid of this person that you despise. It's your chance to get your own back and really break free! £3.99

101 Uses for Granny

"I don't want to be a burden," says Granny. Well, now she won't be. With 101 good uses, you'll wonder how you ever got by before. You can use your Granny to... Warn motorists of your long load... Slow down incoming jets... Mark the fact that you've climbed Everest... Welcome your visitors as a talking doormat... Hold your TV aerial in the best position... and if you are ever short of a Guy in November... £3.99

The Bog Book

MORE HUMOUR TITLES...

The Ancient Art of Farting by Dr. C.Huff

Ever since time began, man (not woman) has farted.
Does this ability lie behind many of the so far
unexplained mysteries of history ?
You Bet - because Dr. C.Huff's research shows
conclusively there's something absolutely rotten
about history taught in schools. If you do most of
your reading on the throne, then this book is your
ideal companion. Sit back and fart yourself silly as
you split your sides laughing! *£3.99*

The Hangover Handbook & Boozer's Bible
(In the shape of a beercan)

Ever groaned, burped and cursed the morning after,
as Vesuvius erupted in your stomach, a bass drum-
mer thumped on your brain and a canary fouled its
nest in your throat? Then you need these 100+
hangover remedies. There's an exclusive Hangover
Ratings Chart, a Boozer's Calendar, a Hangover
Clinic, and you can meet the Great Drunks of History, try the Boozer's Reading Chart, etc., etc. *£3.99*

If you would rather not damage your copy of *The Bog Book*, please use plain paper and remember to include all the details listed below!

Please return to: **Take That Books,
P.O.Box 200, Harrogate, HG1 4XB**

The Bog Book